#GET HIRED

LOOKING FOR JOB IN COVID TIMES, UNLOCK THE SIMPLE & PROVEN PATH TO SURE-SHOT SUCCESS

RAJESH R DHAKTODE

Copyright © Rajesh R Dhaktode
All Rights Reserved.

ISBN 978-1-63957-358-5

This book has been published with all efforts taken to make the material error-free after the consent of the author. However, the author and the publisher do not assume and hereby disclaim any liability to any party for any loss, damage, or disruption caused by errors or omissions, whether such errors or omissions result from negligence, accident, or any other cause.

While every effort has been made to avoid any mistake or omission, this publication is being sold on the condition and understanding that neither the author nor the publishers or printers would be liable in any manner to any person by reason of any mistake or omission in this publication or for any action taken or omitted to be taken or advice rendered or accepted on the basis of this work. For any defect in printing or binding the publishers will be liable only to replace the defective copy by another copy of this work then available.

I dedicate this book to Ms Priyanka Gupta who assisted me in the journey of completing my first book.

Contents

Preface   vii

Acknowledgements   ix

1. Review   1
2. Assessment   4
3. Train   6
4. Visualise   10
5. Getting Ready For The Opportunity   15
6. Practise   19
7. The Slate Is Clean   22

Preface

The Pandemic has been difficult to many people I know. They have lost their livelihood, their enthusiasm their will to survive and are going through difficult times without any guidance or direction.

Having experience of working on a ship I know what happens to the ship which has lost its direction and has no compass to guide it, If not in a good hands such ships will end up sinking or in a shipwreck. This is what will happen to the direction less people who have no silver lining to look at.

With this book I am guiding them for a better future and an engaging and fulfillment present. Both are highly needed in these difficult times.

I Rajesh R Dhaktode feel it is my responsibility as an individual to help the first time workers who are yet to find their first job and also those who have lost or not able to get any job in this challenging times.

With my experience, in Corporate HR and Training, Operations and Business Entrepreneur, I have worn all the caps of an Employee, as an HOD, and an Employer. I can feel the pain at each level. I think I have the right experience to guide the future workforce in purposeful and safe navigation through this pandemic.

I want you to take a pen and paper before starting the first chapter and passionately complete all the activities provided in the chapters. I have written this book in simple English for you to follow the activities. All the activities are powerful tolls for self-improvement and direction. By end of the book you will understand the purpose of each activity; how they help you evolve over a period of time and make you a stronger willed person.

You will also achieve your goal of #Gethired.

Acknowledgements

I acknowledge the support given to me by my family, my friends and my colleagues. In my journey as a trainer to coach to mentor and now a writer, I have been touched with so many passionate human beings who have ignited me to do best in whatever roles I take over.

They say, Life is a journey to enjoy. Hence, I am on a pathway of enjoyment.

CHAPTER ONE

REVIEW

This Chapter is for you to understand the situation you are presently in. The situation with you, and the outside environmental situation. You need to start with a simple basic SWOT Analysis. Where in SWOT stands for

S= Strength – What is good, things that are easy to do.

W= Weakness – having difficulty in this area.

O = Opportunities – Area which has plenty of scopes.

T = Threats – Obstacles, Problems, etc.

These tests you will do first for the outside environment, which means, your neighborhood, city, state, country, etc. Based on your career what do you think is the SWOT for society? You need to understand what's there in the present situation for you. What is happening in your building? Society? The village, Probably your city, maybe what is happening in the state which you are in and maybe in the country in which you reside.

I have provided a block below which I want you to use. You can start with whatever points you quickly start with and try at least to jot down 5 points in each box. If you can think of less than five points in any box need not worry, but think for some time. You need to spend at least five minutes in each box. If need be set a timer for five minutes and spend this five minutes diligently on each box. There is no set sequence, you can start with any box but the idea is to spend at least five minutes in that box and dig deeper to find five points to jot down on the box given below.

SWOT - Analysis of the Outer world.

Strength

1

2

3

4

5

Weakness
1
2
3
4
5

Opportunities
1
2
3
4
5

Threats
1
2
3
4
5

Great, you have done well.

Now think from your perspective, your career, your family, your wishes, your goals, and what you wish to achieve in life. Based on this make another SWOT in the box given below

SWOT - Analysis of your present situation, career, or professional. What have you gained and lost? What are your forthcoming challenges?

Strength
1
2
3
4
5

Weakness
1
2
3
4
5

Opportunities
1

2
3
4
5

Threats
1
2
3
4
5

Based on the SWOT, now you have your areas of Improvement which are weaknesses and areas to tread carefully, which are your threats. This is the time for you to actually work on your weaknesses and threats.

Ideally, you should focus on your strengths and Opportunities in normal times. The present situation is different from the normal times the world has stopped. All activities which happened before the pandemic will take time to start, some may start sooner and some may take time to start. After this pandemic, new opportunities will emerge and thriving opportunities before the pandemic may get shut. When you do both the SWOT tests, both sides become clear to you.

Based on your Inner self SWOT analysis, start working on your problem areas, maybe you have an Anger Management issue, then please read more on how to control your anger or probably get yourself enrolled in an anger management course.

It's time to identify what are your weaknesses and threats and start working on improvising on them.

CHAPTER TWO

ASSESSMENT

We have the SWOT Analysis of the outside environment. In this chapter, we will focus on trying to understand what are the outside environment and opportunities and strengths in the outside environment that you had identified from chapter one.

Presently there are no new shows getting screened on Television, or for that matter, no new movies are getting screened. This throws an opportunity to people who are in the entertainment industry. I know of people who have started following certain personalities on YouTube and other channels, and suddenly many personalities have become famous. Good for them. Netflix, Amazon Prime, and many such screening channels have suddenly increased and they are getting downloaded and watched. This Pandemic has created an opportunity for many such businesses in the Entertainment Industry.

Also as most of the Education is now online, this has thrown many opportunities to those who have moved with time and made their presence felt here in this field. Now you see the Byjus, the Vedantus, and Scholars, etc, trying to increase their presence by advertising and introducing new schemes. You too must have seen many such Education adverts.

I know of few people who have started making videos in these pandemic times. Some are for entertainment, some are for social awareness. Whatever may be their cause this has thrown an opportunity to them. They have not only been engaged but also have become known faces

A person whom I know lost his job went to his village as he could not afford the rent. This was an opportunity for him in disguise as when he went to his village, he saw another threat within the farmers. They had no way to sell their vegetables and fruits and were throwing them or selling them at throwaway prices. This person saw an opportunity and quickly got in touch with his friend and made a simple App by which he could sell his vegetables and fruits through his friends in cities. Presently he has 25,000 to 30,000 households who buy vegetables from his app. Last, when I was speaking to him, this person seemed happy and content in his native place. He does visit the city now but only to grow his business and seek a new opportunity.

While many of the food businesses are closed, one of my friends saw an opportunity in covid times and is now serving covid sumptuous, wholesome meals to patients and relatives. Through this opportunity, he is earning enough to sustain himself during the tough times.

Another person whom I know who is a Hotelier is now relaxed. The reason is, he quickly moved into quarantine accommodation and this seems to be working for him.

In the last few months you may have seen many hobby and training courses going online, do get enrolled in your area of expertise, and keep improving your knowledge associated with your core area. Online courses make you meet new people and get to know them, it's a good way to be in touch with the outside world and meet new people.

Understanding opportunities are the most important aspect, as soon as you identify them half the goal is achieved. You have to execute the idea and work towards benefiting from the opportunity. A benefit not necessary should be from a monetary aspect it can be engagement, recognition, social cause, or any other justification you have for it. Please remember the present times are for you to survive and exist. As and when these days become history, your CV or profile will have an achievement space enhanced as while most of the people who have little to talk about this time you have an achievement in this space.

CHAPTER THREE

TRAIN

Part - 1

I strongly urge you to use this time to the best of the possibility. It is the perfect time to invest in you. Do what you always longed to do, you may not be able to fulfill your wish to visit the Seven Wonders of the World, but from your SWOT Analysis you must have found out what you should be engaged with. If you are still not clear then I urge you to do the SWOT again and this time with a purpose to fulfill your understanding. As, whatever you have done now, will help you in the future course of your career.

Remember Abraham Lincoln's words, if I am given seven hours to cut a tree, I will spend three hours sharpening the axe.

This is the time to invest in you. In tough times most of the achievers have kept their balance by increasing their spiritual quota. It keeps you in check and balance. Along with your spiritual wellbeing you need to keep your physical and mental welling high as well. I have got good peace of mind whenever I do self-affirmations. Self-affirmations are to thank the almighty, the universe, the society and be grateful that he has given you all that many people do not have. You should say that I am the strongest, hardworking, passionate, enthusiastic, and confident at whatever I do. Very soon all my goals are going to be achieved and my dedication will be rewarded. Self-Affirmative talk brings in a lot of peace and calm to the soul and increases your wellbeing quotient.

Read or Listen to positive thoughts and do not get bogged down by what is happening around you. You should listen to music or songs of your favorite performer. The more your mind occupies that there is a problem outside, the more negative you start to get. Media today provides you with details more than required. Also with social media, there is much unverified news that is circulating. This unknowingly affects your mental wellbeing. Hence try not to react to all that you see, hear or read. Keeping calm is difficult but that's what we have to do.

For your mental well-being, four things are very important for you, they are your mantras for fulfillment and happy life. The first is anger management, not to react to any situation. Second, respond; wait before you wish to do something. Understand the consequences and then respond to the situation. Whatever the situation do not lose your sense of humor, keep smiling is your third mantra. Be happy and content in what you have, focus on what you have rather than what you have not. If you have lost someone or something close to your heart, remember the journey with you was destined by the almighty. Spend the time remembering the good times rather than the consequences of the loss, be it situation, person, or anything you possessed or had. Lastly, stress, pressure, tension the more you keep it away, the better for you. It will bring longevity to your life. Your organs will be happy and not fail you.

Your positive frame of mind is more important to be kept now, as this will bring your goal closer to you once we get over these tough times. What is important now is to work on your wholesome wellbeing. Physical wellbeing is most important as results have shown those who exercise regularly are more content and satisfied. Do spend time in exercise, yoga, and meditation. Here when I say exercise it means any physical activity you do in the available confinement. You can surely walk the staircase or walk at home. Many of my friends have not skipped their exercise routine but have modified it to what they can do, and are happy to flaunt f their achievements with their friends. This is another way of being happy and satisfied.

Meditation and Yoga bring along with exercise a favorable glow on your face, and body. When you become comfortable with your body, it increases your confidence. This improves your presentation and your complete wellbeing.

Breathing exercises are a must in daily routines. Experts have said that it increases your capacity of lungs and hence highly recommended.

Then there are things which you always wanted to do, but never had time or resources for it. Well, anything which is engaging, keeping you occupied with a positive frame of mind is highly recommended. As simple as washing dishes, cleaning your cupboard, de-cluttering your house, cooking your favorite dish, trying new recipes, just anything which was not in your normal routine.

This is the time to also gain a new skill set, you always wanted to learn a guitar, maybe draw a painting well go for it. You should use the time to the best of your ability for self-development. Engage yourself in adding skillsets to your profile.

Part -2

Now is the time to get serious about your goals, revisit your goals to see where you stand. The best thing to do is by self-evaluating your goals and achievements, by creating a goal sheet. Most of the professionals in the world use a SMART goal sheet to evaluate their performance. You can use a similar goal sheet for yourself.

The Time tested formula of the SMART goal sheet.

S – Specific – You should be able to write the goal.

M – Measurable – There should be a parameter to measure your goal. (Eg. Loosing 10 Kg's of weight in 3 months)

A – Attainable – This is most important, meaning it should be something which is possible. (eg. – Marrying Mr. or Ms. World. (Is, not a goal.) Marrying a beautiful looking person _____ (Shall be a goal, as it means you should be able to improve or match the person whom you have in mind in various categories such as professional, career, behavioral, social status, looks, etc. to be suitable)

R – Relevant – It should be relevant to you and the purpose you have. (A Visit to planet Mars, may not be a general goal, but if you are a student of astronomy, this can be your goal)

T – Time Bound – Specific by what time frame you shall achieve the goal. In a few of the above examples, the time frame is not mentioned to make it complete you need to add a date to it.

You can also make your goals SMARTER by adding E – for Evaluation and R for Reward.

E – Evaluate. Periodically access your goal sheet to see your progress. Highlight the concern areas in Red, lagging behind in yellow, and on the time frame in green.

R – Review – Reviewing your goal sheet is necessary to be on track.

You can periodically say every three months visit your goal sheet and check your progress.

I have provided below a sample goal sheet that you can use. While using the goal sheet you should visit all the areas which are important for you. (I have given below one example, similarly, prepare your goal sheet keeping in mind the various parameters)

Example

Goal Sheet of _Rajesh R Dhaktode_____

Personal Goal

I, Rajesh wish to write a book on self-development and self-help which will be a guiding tool to all those who wish to get a job or work and make a sparkling career in their field of activity by May '21.

Goal Sheet of (your name) _____

Personal Goal

Academic Goal

Behavioral Goal

Career or Professional Goal

Any other area/parameter relevant for you

Once you are clear of your goals, it prepares your training sheet. This training sheet should be used by you to complete areas of improvement. I strongly suggest you check your goal sheet daily. You should paste or keep the goal sheet handy or in the vicinity where at least once in a day you are able to see it. This assures you and motivates you to take step towards the achievement of your goals, which is training self or working towards your aim, goal, etc.

Eg. If you aim is to become Manager of the department you should work towards finding out what all manager needs to know to perform. If Excel skills are relevant, your Training sheet should have excellence in Excel mentioned. To become proficient in Excel you should either learn through books, search in Google steps to improve your excel skills. It will throw many options in front of you. You can either take online or offline if possible classes to improvise your excel skills.

CHAPTER FOUR

VISUALISE

This chapter tells you more about achieving. That is visualizing your achievement. Close your eyes and now think you have already achieved your goals. If your goal was to get hired as a Manager, or become an IPS Officer or get into Civil services administration or for that matter getting into B School for learning, etc. visualize that you have already achieved it. Think that you are in the chair of the Manager or Head of Department, which you wanted to become. Now visualize a normal routine of yourself. How will you start your day, what activities you will do to justify the role?

To make this step work your visualization has to be strongest as if you are leaving the moment. You should see yourself, from top to bottom completely groomed for the role for which you aimed for. Once in the role leave the moment from morning to evening. Visualize yourself performing the daily task of the role. You should be able to see yourself doing your daily normal activities and job related to the role. Visualize yourself having a team meeting where you have delivered a starling speech on the performance of your department or section. Try to remember the brief you spoke to your staff. Also, visualize yourself meeting your superior over a tea and discussing the progress yourself. Remember what you heard and what you spoke or answered have a proper dialogue. For this, you can have your own storyline which you have visualized.

The next step is to open your eyes and with a pen and paper start jotting down all the activities you did while in the role. What all you felt while you were in the role of your achievement? Did it elevate you, or were you struggling to speak or perform your duties? Whatever you may have visualized, do write it down. Note as much as possible, think hard, and do justice to the writing, Best sequence will be to start from the morning to night and write down the complete storyline you visualized. You need to add your feelings, what you wore, and what you saw yourself as.

Once you have noted down all the points you could think of you can close the paper. Take few breaths maybe a glass of water and take a walk or listen to music or play with your toddler or pet. Just detach and don't think of the visualization for some time. This process is called calibration of the mind. As you went to a stage of performance and then noted down the performance. Now is the time to detach from it and get out of that zone.

Once you are completely out and have no thoughts of your process you can now visit the worksheet you wrote the details. This process may take a day. So best is the next day when you are completely out of the zone. Read what you have written and observe yourself. As now you are in the present moment and not in the future you will be able to do know what all you wish to do or achieve to live the role you visited.

Once you are clear of thoughts you should now start writing down from the present path which you are and the future path which you will visit what all improvements or shortcomings you need to overcome.

Say if you wanted to earn a role in NASA or ISRO, you need to have besides Education a certain personality and Training for the role. Similarly, a Lawyer, A Doctor, an HR Professional, or a Sales and Marketing professional have their own needs and wants of performance. If You wish to be hired by a B School or for that matter any particular school, college or Institute globally start working on understanding their parameters of hiring.

#BeHired works at its best when you take the pain to understand the prerequisite of the role you wished to be hired. Today with the net, and all information available at the click of the button nothing is far from you. Visit the website of the company you wish to join, or the place you wish to work, or the job you wish to get. Read, Learn gather information or maybe go through a proper Job Description of the role. One of my known people referred his son to me for help. This young chap was unsuccessful in getting the job which he wished for, He was a technical graduate and all the roles offered to him were in Marketing, Sales or Data collection. He was devastated and felt his education which he worked hard on was getting injustice. When I started speaking to him, what I could sense was that the person over a period of time has become difficult to speak, before you could start the conversation he would say why he does not like data collection or roaming around the city. I could understand his anger and once he finished his tale, I made him go through the similar exercise I defined in the above paragraphs.

I asked him to take a seat and visualize as if he is working in a Production team as a preventive maintenance team worker. I made him close his eyes and go through the complete process of visualization of his role. I also asked him to play the role from morning till evening and define his feelings. Here I was noting down what he was saying. We completed this exercise over a period of time. Meanwhile, I was his writer, and whatever I questioned him or asked him he answered me while he was actually downing a cap of a maintenance technician. At the end of the session, we had tea and with a promise that he will come again to visit me tomorrow, and he left.

The next day as decided the young chap came to me and was a different person, he was more gentle more docile and his etiquettes were different from what I had seen the first day. Over a coffee, we started the conversation and I asked him to read what I had jotted down. As he started reading his face lit and tears started flowing through his eyes. With great difficulty, he was hiding his wet eyes but kept reading what I had written. "In my blue clean overall, I started my day with a briefing from my superiors, where I was told to follow a senior technician. We went around the plant oiling and greasing the machines and my new safety shoes started crumbling as I was bending over the machines and stretching to reach the top pipe. All this he had visualized with my basic prompting. By the end of the session, he also read that his overall was wet, from sweat and oily and greasy, and needed a wash.

When the exercise got over the young chap again trying hard to hide his tears was desperately asking me how he liked to live the role. We again sat again together this time with a purpose to find out what he should do to get into such a role, with my experience I guided him and made him understand that while he had the right education and profile the reason he was not getting into his desired role was that his ability to express his wishes. Now with the experience of visualizing behind his back, he immediately made his own goal and training sheet and with a promise that he will be disciplined in his approach henceforth, we parted.

In a few days' time, I received a thanksgiving call from my friend saying what all education could not achieve, has been achieved over a couple of days in my mentoring session. He was happy that his son had been selected in one of the prestigious organizations as a Trainee in his desired department. He had been hired.

Most of the time we fail to see what is obvious and hence it is necessary to visit the drawing boards and revisit our goals from time to time. Here

I wish to tell you about a challenging situation of a person who wished to work in a particular company/organization. The person had good years of experience down his belt and had failed to understand why he was not getting success in various attempts which he tried to apply for a cruise ship job. Through a known friend he was referred to me and over a discussion over a phone he sent me his CV / Bio-data. As soon as I saw his CV I knew the problem area.

In the last four years, he had moved five companies. As promised to him, I texted him to meet me on a certain day, and time. We talked about here and there and about his education, experience and generally, I found the person was good at his job and could have easily made it to the cruise liners. While discussing the person said how his all known friends were in this organization and were doing well, earning in Pounds for similar working hours he was putting in India.

This was troubling him and the cause of his pain. Without saying anything, I spoke to him about my process and he was happy to go through it. I made him visualize life on a cruise ship and was surprised to know that he knew a lot about the role, courtesy of his friends. While he was visualizing I noted few points for him and at the end of the session, we decided to meet on a certain day as he had duties to attend.

On the particular date, the gentlemen were before time and waiting for me in my office. We spoke about here and there and over a hot sipping tea, I opened his visualization notes. As he started reading he was delighted and happy to see that he was on board, he was enjoying the read and had a big smile all over his face.

At the end of the session, we did our goal and training sheet, it was time for me now to confront and make him understand that his too many job switching was costing him a role at sea. I made him understand, and for this purpose, I had to put him in the shoe of the Employer. Will he as an Employer, hire a person who was moving a lot, here too he was justifying the switch saying for a bigger role, better salary, I made the moves. He was missing the point.

Somehow I made him understand how an international Employer will hire him if working in India itself he was not able to work for more than one year in any one particular organization.

This logic was difficult for him to digest. Slowly he was able to accept his mistake and made a promise to me and himself that he will not move at least for two years from the present place of work. I was not sure he would stick to his words as he had mentioned to me that he was getting another offer for a better role and salary, but not a cruise job while we were chatting in our earlier meeting.

He refined his goal sheet and training sheet and now had written that in the next two years he will stick to one place and then on a particular date he will apply again for the cruise ship job.

I had forgotten the episode and then on one fine day, I was surprised to see a message on what Sapp coming from an unknown number. This person was saying thanks to me and that he was selected for a cruise job role and was visiting the office to start his visa and other process and he wanted my guidance. I ignored the message as his name was missing and he was not on my contact list.

The next day, I received a call from this particular person, and as he says I am so and so things become evident to me. I congratulated him on his achievement and wished him all the best and inquired about how he made it. He over the phone told me how he used to see the goal sheet as and when the thought of changing jobs came to him. Somehow he managed to work in a present organization for almost 20 months after which he applied for a cruise job and was surprised to get a call for an Interview. I was happy for him, that the person accomplished his goal and got hired.

CHAPTER FIVE

GETTING READY FOR THE OPPORTUNITY

In this chapter, we will get ourselves prepared for any forthcoming opportunity. Yes, you read right, getting prepared from the perspective that all your tools for facing any opportunity are sharpened and ready to use.

Let's understand what you need to keep ready.

Bio-data / CV or Curriculum Vitae / Profile / Resume / Work History / Life History all these terms you may have heard and must be wondering how are they different. Well to make your life easier, all are the same. Those things which you wish to inform the prospective Employer.

You may have seen various new formats of CV. In my experience and also what I have gathered information from the various HR or Hiring agencies the best Profile is short and to the point giving all necessary information about the candidate.

I have seen profiles that are made and every time a person leaves the job, he just adds to the pages. So in twenty years, a person may have a 20-page Resume. While the candidate is trying to be honest and giving all the desired information, please understand the Employer is not interested in long CVs. In fact, such CVs do not even reach Employers; they are weeded out by HR personnel. So the challenge is how to make your profile Interesting that it reaches the right person and you get a call for an Interview.

To assist you I have provided below a basic format you can use to update your resume, to make it interesting

BIODATA

Basic Information – Name and Surname, Address, Contact details, Email id

Photo – Small size face cutout.

Basic Summary of Profile – Two lines for first-time appliers, three to five lines for experience with five to ten years.

For more than 20 years of experience, the maximum summary should not be more than 10 to 12 lines. Highlighting creativity and achievements.

First-time workers should mention their Education in the next field and those who are experienced should start with explaining the work experience. Experienced should highlight major achievements in profile.

Work experience starting from the present and then previous.

For Profile which has more than 20 years experience, should highlight and describe maximum last three work experience and rest all experiences can be defined in one-liner along with Month and the year of joining and leaving.

Make a small tabulation for core skillsets, Communication, level of usage of Excel, power-point, or any other usage of computer assisting you in the role which you have applied for. E.g. AutoCAD for Architecture or Civil Engineers.

Give a brief of your Academic achievement along with ratings and year of passing out is needed, or years of course eg. Graduate in Arts – English '02 to 05 (Makes it clear that you completed the course in three years denoting last year was passing out the year)

Any Training or extracurricular activity details, hobby if related to the role you are applying for.

Name and

Make effort to make your CV presentable, a maximum of two to three pages. Use pictorials to mention your experience at various organizations.

We also have recently seen trends of Presentation CV and also Video CV's

Presentation CV is summarizing your CV in, animated, pictorial, or with photographs making it more interesting for a viewer.

Video CV – It is normally an add-on and is more of an attachment to the Presentation of a pdf or photograph CV. It basically tells the viewer more about the person, as he may be able to see, hear and get more information through body language, facial expression, and eyes about the candidate. It is used normally in front of the house hire.

Now a day's people are also using video CVs if they come from a skill set area, like say magician, cooking, etc.

In today's world, you cannot ignore digital media, so the best is to update your Linkedin, FB, and Instagram profiles. Keeps your tweeter account following the think tanks and experts in your area of operation. Linkedin is most favored for Professional introduction so keep it updated and do not mix it for the social messaging platform. You can use it to connect with professionals, experts, and HR recruiters, hiring agencies if you are looking to #gethired.

Other most important things which HR and Evaluator look at in a CV are the gaps. You should have proper justification for the gaps and be able to prove what kept you occupied during the time. Even in this Pandemic period, I would urge readers to update their CV and mention a couple of lines on how you had kept yourselves engaged & occupied in this period, what skillsets you added to your profile. Etc.

I here would like to give an example of how a Recruiter or HR person works when he is shortlisting various profiles. Imagine an HR who is filling a vacancy for a Salesforce team. The HR needs to get few CVs and to get few CVs they need to advertise the vacancy. The person may use digital media, newspaper advertising, social sites like Naukri, Monster, etc. or it may internally in the organization send a circular informing or urging people to spread the news of the vacancy.

Depending on the organization and the scale of pay, there will be few profiles coming to the HR Person. Now the person suppose has received 20 applications for say one role. That means the person has to evaluate all profiles to get a suitable profile closer as per the Job Description or the role description. The HR person must have got a small brief on the suitability of a person and must have created a bullet point framework. He or she will go through all the profiles and check their relevance against the bullet point and highlight those CVs.

Most of the hiring people find it difficult to go through long CVs. In this scenario, how will your CV stand out? Simple if you have followed my previous instructions your profile will be easily shortlisted provided it suits the Job Description.

Hence it is a must to create a first and lasting impression with your CV.

Many Applicants forget to attach a Forward Application letter. For senior positions, the application letter is a must. Please create your application letter in a simple user-friendly format. It should not be more than one pager and should highlight the position you are applying for and why you think are suitable for the position. To crack this test, readers should highlight their achievements only. The rest of the Information anyway is again available in Bio-data.

As and when the opportunity arises, an updated CV mentioning what has been your achievement in this pandemic period will be picked first than any other CV. You will always have an edge as you have started where the other Profiles have ended. Most CVs will say I worked till March '20 and was given a break or laid off. It's a known thing that many jobs have become redundant in this pandemic and those who were holding this position were laid off.

The person who has gainfully utilized this period will come out positive and will be Hired.

CHAPTER SIX

PRACTISE

Practice makes a person perfect

So in this chapter, I will talk about how you should be prepared for the next step which is the Interview. If you have followed the steps I have proposed in this book, you should be sooner than later facing an Interview panel. This is the time for you to shine and come out with flying colors.

Most of the Interviewers are trying their best to find the most suitable person for any role which they wish to hire. For it they will always go wider, meaning spreading the word more so that more people will apply for the role. The profiles which they have liked will be highlighted and get a call for an Interview. If you are preparing for any tests or for that matter civil services, or any preparatory exam leading to a job, your half preparation is done till you get a call for an Interview. I have seen many people forget this process and leave it to their guts or god to help them in the process.

Depending on the organization, seniority of the role, individual contributor to team contributor, etc. Interviews these days are using new techniques to reach the best three candidates for the role. Most Interviews you must have known are

Telephonic Interview – Interview over a phone, mostly only speaking and listening, and widely used for the first phase of Interview.

Video Interview – Most favored in this time wherein you see and listen to a person live over zoom or Skype call. Google meet and teams are also there so in case if you are getting ready for any of these kinds of Interviews please understand the usage of the application. Register yourself in advance and ask someone to guide you and make you familiar.

Face to Face Interview – Here you will be meeting the person who is going to Interview you. F2F Interview is widely used for selection of the candidates. F2F Interview has many structured Interviews which we will now understand.

Panel Interview – You have a group of people in The Interview, Like CEO, HR, Sales Head, Training, etc.

Group Interview – Group Interview is where many candidates are interviewed at a similar time. This technique is used when you wish to hire first-time workers. Group Discussion, minute talk, etc, are normally used in this technique.

Behavioral Event Interview – This Interviewing technique is used when you wish to know more about an episode or a thing that has happened in past.

Stress Interview – Ideally a stress Interview is done when the role needs higher patience. A stress Interview is basically you are asked uncomfortable questions and your reaction is observed. In many consulates, Visa officers use these techniques when they Interview a candidate applying for Visa.

Competency-Based interview – This Interview is mostly structured to understand the skill set of the candidate. Eg. You ask a Cook or a Chef to prepare a dish to see his competency in preparing the dish. A person driving skills are tested by asking him to drive any particular vehicle. The technique is used mostly for skill-based hiring.

In Basket technique – Giving various assignments to a person and based on priority check the response of the person on how he or she is able to take multiple tasks and priorities the tasks. This technique is more comfortable for senior roles, or any role which needs a high level of understanding of the urgency and important things Personal Assistant to an MD or Director, etc.

As you are now aware of the various techniques for Interviewing, you should also be aware of how to perform better in each Interviewing pattern. The reason I have defined this chapter as Practise because Driving cannot be learned by just reading or for that matter swimming cannot be learned unless getting your body wet, so to perform better you need to practice, practice and practice.

When you get into any language test, especially those who evaluate your skills on various parameters such as listening, Speaking, Writing, and Reading you will learn in the journey to focus on all parameters and not one. Eg. IELTS test for English Language OET is another Language test for Healthcare Language training. Similarly, most of the language training in the world follows a similar pattern, Practice practice and practice for various scenarios to be perfect.

You must have seen many B Schools focusing on the art of Interviewing as they have understood that with the right direction their candidates perform better in the Campus placements hence many have introduced Campus to Corporate bridge-building courses wherein they focus on these skillsets. In fact, in the last semester, most of the management schools focus more on these parameters. If you have been trained in such a B school, you will surely do well In Interviews. Those who have not been recently trained or are looking to get hired need to practice more.

There are many online courses which will help you improve your skillset, Like the art of speaking, Art of Interviewing, etc. In our Academy, we too run a similar program to focus on the wholesome development of the people.

You can also speak to your HR friends or your coach, mentor, guide, teacher, etc, and ask them to help you in this area. Ask them to conduct mock Interviews for you. The more you practice the more you get better at this.

In the whole world not many have had a chance to get interviewed in this pandemic period, so whatever practice you do will help you get to your goal closer. In this case, it is #gethired.

Many companies focus on Psychometric tests to hire the final candidates. A Psychometric test was basically started o find out inner traits of people which are not visible. To summarize it, we can say the mental wellbeing of a person. As we have seen in the earlier chapters how important it is to keep your mental wellbeing along with spiritual and physical wellbeing. If you have followed the guidance steps provided in the chapters you will easily scale through these tests.

Most of the companies who use these tests don't do it to reject a candidate, but to finalize a candidate from the few shortlisted.

You too can practice psychometric tests online, there are few free versions available along with the results of the test. It may help you to understand your underlying dominating traits.

CHAPTER SEVEN

THE SLATE IS CLEAN

In case if you have lost your job due to a pandemic or were not able to find the right matching job during this time please remember the world is slowly healing. Sooner or Later all the Economic activities will start, it may get time to get back to pre covid times but the direction is clear.

Just as you have gone through the tough times, the Employer has gone through the tough times. Organizations will slowly start picking people to increase their market share. As they know the slate is clean and now big or small, all are standing in one line. Whatever experience they had was before Pandemic. Post - pandemic all are equal and hence they will quickly start increasing the market share. The first ones to find the jobs will be Sales and Marketing team members, followed by other departments.

Whatever your role, you should be ready to #gethired sooner.

Employers who are reviving their organizations will be designing safe parameters for revival. HR people and senior team members will play a pivotal role in the revival strategy. The strategy will be based on quick re-bouncing and short-term plans, which will scale to a longer vision. You may find work, but may not be happy with the pay scales. My suggestion to you is not to worry about the remuneration or salary. Getting on the right Train is more important now rather than the scale of pay and salary. If you are in the right direction, other things will fall in place. (This means compromising on your salary, When you start a job your parameter should not be pre-covid salary. Try to be realistic in your approach. Employers may also put a certain % of salary as a performance allowance. Whatever strategy they use please remember your mission is to #gethired)

Employees this day do not value, the safety of the organization, leadership, ethics, vision, direction, focus, etc. Covid times have shown the organization with strong values has existed and rests have perished. Now is the time for you to value these parameters.

I also wish to mention here, Newton's Laws of force, Inertia, and the second Mass into acceleration. The same will be applicable post-covid. As long as you are in the right place, time will reveal a favorable destiny. This means you will get into a better situation, once the economy picks up.

All the previous chapters in this book have been speaking on your wholesome wellbeing. The reason you have been hired is due to your high empathy. The new hiring parameters designed by the Employers have picked you keeping this in mind. They want a person with high enthusiasm, passion, dedication, and confidence.

All this has been the outcome of the activities we learned and followed in various chapters.

With a new enthusiasm, create your path and tread well. Accomplish your goals in a systematic approach; apply all your personal learning's on the job. Your hard work, efforts will take your organization to newer achievements, which will further grow your skillsets.

While we have come to the end of the final chapter, please remember we are still in the midst of a crisis. Pandemic Is not coming to end as yet. This also means you have time to follow all the activities I have designed for you.

If you wish to create a better future, get on the journey of wholesome well-being, and #gethired.

www.ingramcontent.com/pod-product-compliance
Lightning Source LLC
Chambersburg PA
CBHW020715180526
45163CB00008B/3098